Gallery Books
Editor: Peter Fallon

MOUNT EAGLE

John Montague

"MOUNT EAGLE

Gallery Books

Mount Eagle
is first published
simultaneously in paperback
and in a clothbound edition
on 24 November 1988.

The Gallery Press
Loughcrew
Oldcastle
County Meath
Ireland

© John Montague 1988

ISBN 1 85235 030 X (*paperback*)
     1 85235 031 8 (*clothbound*)

The Gallery Press receives financial assistance from An Chomhairle Ealaíon / The Arts Council, Ireland, and acknowledges also the assistance of the Arts Council of Northern Ireland in the publication of this book.

Contents

Acknowledgements

'Migrant Poet' was translated by John Montague and Donncha Ó Corráin.

Nuala Ní Dhomhnaill's poem, 'An Bhabóg Bhriste', appears in *Féar Suaithinseach*, An Sagart, Maynooth, 1984.

Acknowledgements are due to the editors and publishers of *Antaeus, Aquarius, Bitter Harvest* (Scribners), *Cahiers sur la Poèsie* (Presses Universitaires de Bordeaux), *Encounter, Exile* (Toronto), *The Honest Ulsterman, The Irish Press, The Irish Times, Krino, The Malahat Review* (Canada), *The New Nation, The New Statesman, North Dakota Quarterly, Orbis, Ploughshares, Poetry Australia, The Sunday Tribune, Temenos, The Bright Wave/An Tonn Gheal* (Raven Arts Press) and *The Quarryman* (UCC) in which some of these poems have appeared.

A selection was published in *Firebird* (Penguin), *La Lange Greffée* (Editions Belin, Paris) and *Amours, marées* (William Blake, Bordeaux).

'Crossing' and 'The Leap' were first published in a limited edition by The Deerfield Press, Massachusetts, and The Gallery Press.

for E. O. S.

Pacific Legend

In their houses beneath the sea
the salmon glide, in human form.

They assume their redgold skin
to mount the swollen stream,

Wild in the spawning season;
a shining sacrifice for men!

So throw back these bones again:
they will flex alive, grow flesh

When the ruddy salmon returns,
a lord to his underwater kingdom.

Up So Doün

I open underwater eyes
and the great lost world
of the primordial drifts
a living thicket of coral
a darting swarm of fish

> (*or the moon with an apron*
> *of iceblue tinted cloud,*
> *rust bright Mars or Saturn's*
> *silvery series of spheres*)

how quiet it is down here
where wandering minnows explore
the twin doors of my eyelids
lip silently against my mouth

> (*how still it is up here*
> *where I dance quietly to myself,*
> *stilt across a plain, hardly*
> *disturbing the dust on the moon's shelf*)

I had forgotten that we live between
gasps of, glimpses of miracle;
once sailed through the air like birds,
walked in the waters like fish.

Springs

for Ted Hughes

Dying, the salmon
heaves up its head
in the millstream.
Great sores ring
its gills, its eyes,
a burning rust
slowly corrodes
the redgold skin.

Great river king,
nearby the Nore pours
over foaming weirs
its light and music,
endlessly dissolving
walls into webs of
water that drift away
among slow meadows.

But you are abdicating,
you are yielding,
no fight left but in
the hinge of your jaws,
(the hook or *kype*)
gasping, clasping
for a last breath
of this soiled kingdom.

Prince of ocean, from
what shared springs
we pay you homage
we have long forgotten

but I mourn your passing
and would erase
from this cluttered earth
our foul disgrace:

Drain the poison
from the streams,
cleanse the enormous
belly of ocean, tear
those invisible miles
of mesh so that your
kin may course again
through clear waters.

Moving In

The world we see only shadows
what was there. So a dead man
fables in your chair, or stands
in the space your table now holds.
Over your hearth the sea hisses
and a storm wind harshly blows.
Before your eyes the red sandstone
of the wall crumbles, weed run wild
where three generations ago
a meadow climbed, above a city
which now slowly multiplies,
its gaunt silos, fuming mills
strange to the first inhabitants
as Atlantis to a fish's eyes.

Grattan Hill, 1974

Hearth Song

for Seamus Heaney

1

The Nialls' cottage had one:
it lived under a large flagstone,
loving the warmth of the kitchen.

Chill or silent, for whole days,
it would, all of a sudden, start
its constant, compelling praise.

And all of us, dreaming or chatting
over the fire, would go quiet,
harkening to that insistent creak,

Accustoming ourselves all over again
to that old, but always strange sound,
coming at us from under the ground,

Rising from beneath our feet,
welling up out of the earth,
a solitary, compulsive song

Composed for no one, a tune
dreamt up under a flat stone,
earth's fragile, atonal rhythm.

2

And did I once glimpse one?
I call up that empty farmhouse,
its blind, ghostly audience

And a boy's bare legs dangling
down from a stool, as he peers
through a crack in the flagstones

And here it strikes up again,
that minute, manic cellist,
scraping the shape of itself,

Its shining, blue-black back
and pulsing, tendril limbs
throbbing and trembling in darkness

a hearth song of happiness.

Postmistress: A Diptych

1. *Brigid Montague* (*1876-1966*)
A hand pushes back a wisp of gray hair.
All day people come to complain and take.
She stands at her desk, signing, listening;
Oldfashioned wire-rimmed spectacles glint.
Worn rights of way to well or bog,
Protracted, hurtful family quarrels,
The resentment of the trapped animal,
Shouldering others on their narrow path;
To bear that always renewed burden,
The tuneless cries of the self-absorbed,
And stand patient, serving under the yoke,
Never complaining: always ready to assist;
Bow down, for your own sake, before the good,
Their sweet assurance, taken for granted.

2. *Winifred Montague* (*1900-1983*)
Old girl courier of Cumann na mBan,
Even before you died you were on cloud nine,
Squatting like an effigy of yourself
In your comfortable rocking chair
With an aureole of white, wispy hair.
Not a sign of contrariness, of bad temper
Anywhere! Faltering old neighbours or
Protestants you rarely had a good word for
Greeted with benevolence; or benign indifference?
On the mantelpiece burly Pope John Paul
Shared his public place of honour
With your life's monarch: the Queen Mother.
Such rich acceptance might take care
Of our little local spot of bother.

Foreign Field

for Edna Longley

Paddy's whole place was a clearing house:
A public 'phone in the hallway,
Folk huddled around a tiled fireplace.

But we were given tea in the front parlour,
Chill as the grave, a good place to talk,
Among brass trinkets, Long Kesh harps.

A patrol catwalks through the garden.
'You can see how we are being protected,'
Paddy jokes, with a well-rehearsed laugh.

A single shot. 'Jesus, that was close!'
The whole patrol crouches to the grass,
Though one slumps. 'Your man's hurt.

You don't take cover with your rifle
Between your legs, like starting to dive.
Let's way out and see if he's alive.'

All the soldier barked was 'Freeze!'
But Paddy led us to where he lay,
A chubby lad, only about eighteen,

That hangdog look, hair close-cropped,
Surplus of a crowding England, now
Dying in a puddle of wet and blood.

And still the soldier: 'Don't move!'
Paddy ran back in to fetch some linen.
'Don't touch him!' He kneels down

To cover his skull gently, a broken egg.
'When a man's got, he's a non-combatant,'
Paddy apologises, shepherding us inside.

An hour later, an army ambulance raced up,
An army doctor leaps down. Out playing
Again, the children chant: 'Die, you bastard!'

Next morning, they checked out the area.
Someone had pruned an old tree in a garden,
Opening a new line of fire, instead.

Semiotics

Loudest of all our protests when
the Deaf Mute Club of Ireland gather
to honour a brother, slammed down
by a plastic bullet, near his Council home.
Challenged, he could only wave to answer
some tense and trigger-happy soldier.
Upon the broad British Embassy steps
the spokesman of the Deaf Mutes
makes an impassioned, fiery speech
in sign language. Fierce applause.
What officials spy through windows
of those comfortable Georgian rooms
is a flickering semaphore of fingers,
then an angry swirl of palms.

Cassandra's Answer

1
All I can do is curse, complain.
I told you the flames would come
and the small towns blaze. Though

Precious little you did about it!
Obdurate. Roots are obstructions
as well as veins of growth.

How my thick tongue longs
for honey's ease, the warm
full syllables of praise

Instead of this gloomy procession
of casualties, clichés of decease;
deaf mutes' clamouring palms.

To have one subject only,
fatal darkness of prophecy,
gaunt features always veiled.

I have forgotten how I sang
as a young girl, before my voice
changed, and I tolled funerals.

I feel my mouth grow heavy again,
a storm cloud is sailing in;
a street will receive its viaticum

in the fierce release of a bomb.
Goodbye, Main Street, Fintona,
goodbye to the old Carney home.

2
To step inside a childhood home,
tattered rafters that the dawn
leaks through, brings awareness

Bleaker than any you have known.
Whole albums of Births, Marriages,
roomfuls of tears and loving confidences

Gone as if the air has swallowed them;
stairs which climb towards nothing,
walls hosed down to flaking stone:

you were born inside a skeleton.

A Real Irishman

On St. Patrick's Day, Billy Davidson cried,
Big and blubbering, by the rock garden.
The master had ordered him to play outside,
Snapping, 'You're not a real Irishman,
You're a Protestant'. I slip out to comfort
Big Billy, chance an arm around him.
'What does it matter, your religion –
Some people still call me the American! –
What counts most is, you're my friend.'
Decades later, in a dark pub, after hours,
A swirl of trouble with two off-duty U.D.R.
Suddenly in the background, a rough voice roars:
'John Montague is my old friend and neighbour;
Lay a hand on him and you deal with Billy Davidson'.

Respect

Thady, sixty years out of Donegal,
propped, overflowing his tall barstool,
my father's pal, the last, hollering:

'Jim was a decent man, he prayed every night
for his family; I'm glad to meet his son.
Sure, he took the drop, but never gave in.'

(They shared a horsebox in a Brooklyn slum,
a boarding house run by rheumatic Mrs Averril
who pitted her rosary against the Atom Bomb.)

'But your uncle was a right whoremaster,
riding black women.' Monaghan's father
snorts in the background, 'Keep the party clean'.

Just as our ears were beginning to burn!
Thady, an old motor man, reverses gears,
rewinding the thread of those solitary years

To recall a summer evening in Donegal,
how he won the raffle in the Parish Hall.
First prize: a kiss from the prettiest girl.

His eyes moisten, his voice thickens,
he lays aside his daily, *Journal American*,
'I can still picture her shy expression'.

Among gasoline fumes, run-down brownstones,
Thady still holds on to his lucky number,
waiting stolidly on the platform beside her,

How when he kissed her, there was a cheer.
'The one time in my whole life.' Thoughtfully,
Thady looks back down into his chilled beer.

'But I have always respected women.
So did your father.' The stale odour
of lives broken down, next to nothing,

yet, on the litter, that stray offering.

Husbandry

for Derry Jeffares

Because you were barren,
male by male tree, or
one female by another,
I had to cut you down.
A hard task, kneeling with
the saw's serrated blade,

To scythe thick grass,
seek out your smothered side.
Close to earth as possible,
the gardening manual said;
a neighbouring appletree
shook petals on my head –
to see an old neighbour
so roughly treated?

A bird called and called,
balanced upon a thorn,
a spider crawled upon
my sweating hand until
the foot was sawn, and
all your branching platform

Swayed: but still held on.
I had to put both arms
around your lean waist
to tug you finally down.
No damp pith spirted,
but that raw stump shone.

A Sharpening Stone

That rasping sound;
Someone cleansing metal,
Scouring a saucepan, sets
Memory's teeth on edge;
A sharpening stone.

Joe MacKenna rubs, runs
The ball of his thumb
Along the stalk tangled blade,
Shrugs, finding no edge.
He leans down to lift
The gray grained cylinder
Under a coltsfoot leaf
Or a cap's sweatband.

He plants the scythe tip
Firmly in the earth,
Then begins to strop
Both sides of the blade
With a caressing slide
Until its crescent arc
Glints like a scimitar.

Now Joe fires the big stone
Back into its corner,
Spits on both palms
Before he grasps
Those two curved handles
And turns in to confront
The nodding heads of corn:
Work yet to be done.

Turnhole

We part the leaves.

Small, squat, naked
Jim Toorish stood in
the churning middle
of Clarkes' turnhole.

Black hair on his poll,
a roll of black hair
over his stomach, that
strange tussock below.

With a rib of black
fur along his back
from thick neckbone
to simian buttocks.

From which – *inescapable* –
his father root sprang,
gross as a truncheon,
normal as a pump-handle.

And cheerfully splashing,
scooping chill waters over
his curls, his shoulders –
that hairy thing!

To cleanse everything
but our prurient giggling
which took long years
for me to exorcise

Until I saw him again,
upright and glorious,
a satyr, laughing in
the spray at Florence.

Sheela na Gig

The bloody tent-flap opens. We slide
into life, slick with slime and blood.
Cunt, or Cymric *cwm*, Chaucerian *quente*,
the first home from which we are sent
into banishment, to spend our whole life
cruising to return, raising a puny mast
to sail back into those moist lips
that overhang *labia minora* and *clitoris*.
To sigh and die upon the Mount of Venus,
layer after layer of warm moss,
to return to that first darkness!
Small wonder she grins at us, from gable
or church wall. For the howling babe
life's warm start: man's question mark.

Gabriel

To encounter an archangel
demands no preparation, although
frail the will, weak the vessel.
You hardly notice his wings,
falcon wide, or warmly folded,
for he was always expected. And
your healed heart trembles.
In the teeth of the hurricane,
sing sweetness, he announces,
in the pitch of this darkness,
sing tenderness, and if you will,
as omen for the imminent world,
sing peace. The dove's breast
stirs in the savour of his presence.

Fair Head

Night after night
we lay, embracing,
under the shadows
of Sir John's Castle.

Or in the hedge
by the lodge gates
– Maureen Canavan –
arms straining

towards a freedom
neither of us felt
willing to mention:
abhorred temptation!

Hugging and kissing
but holding our lower
parts separate and
rigid as gateposts

leading to adventures
we could never enter
blithely together;
love's untilled estate

in moonlight around us,
from cobwebbed cellars
the mocking laughter
of a ghostly landlord.

Tonguetied I felt
you drift away, with
nothing done or said,
only the lost fragrance

of your fair head –
ceannbhán, a bog blossom –
on warm summer evenings
along the Waterside

or bent towards mine
in Glencull choir
as the handbell shivers
O Salutaris Hostia.

Deer Park

A flourish of silver
trumpets as the royal
favourite is prepared
for the swansdown bed.

Fingers and toes
palpable, succulent
as those pert curves
of mouth, snub nose.

The string of pearls
on her stomach folds
luminously pendent
like rare raindrops

While a pair of pure-
bred hunting hounds
snuffle her plump
and perfumed hands.

A candid light streams
from such guileless,
dimpled nakedness, such
cherubic openness!

And the fillet of
gold she bears so
demurely in honour
of her sovereign master,

Upon her piled strands
of auburn Irish hair,
looped to reveal her
golden neck collar.

A king's treasure
of roseate flesh
caught on canvas
for a king's pleasure

With a full quiver
of arrows, a dangling
brace of pheasant
all stamped: royal property.

Matins

That final bright morning you climb
The stairs to my balcony bed,
Unasked; unashamed: naked.
Barely a please was said
But in the widening light
Our bodies linked, blazed,
Our spirits melded. The dawn
Of a capital city swarmed
Beneath us, but we were absorbed,
Your long hair tenting your head,
Your body taut as a divining rod.
There is in such exchanges a harvest,
A source or wellspring of sweetness,
Grace beyond sense, body's intelligence.

Crossing

Your lithe and golden body
haunts me, as I haunt you:
corsairs with different freights
who may only cross by chance
        on lucky nights.

So our moorings differ.
But scents of your pleasure
still linger disturbingly
around me: fair winds or
        squalls of danger?

There is a way of forgetting you,
but I have forgotten it:
prepared wildly to cut free,
to lurch, like a young man,
        towards ecstasy!

Nightly your golden body turns
and turns in my shuddering dream.
Why is the heart never still,
yielding again to the cardinal
        lure of the beautiful?

Age should bring its wisdom
but in your fragrant presence
my truths are one, swirling
to a litany – sweet privateer –
        of grateful adulation.

The Leap

This journey I have made
a leap backwards in time,
headstrong as a young man,
against all warnings.

1
Memories of leaping
the Garvaghey river
on summer evenings
during long holidays.

Sounds enlarged through
the deepening twilight:
Clarkes calling cattle
to sway to their byre,

A bucket clanging.
Enclosed in that warm
web of sounds, details
amplified by distance.

The lengthy run-up
– muscles tensing –
to sail over the
slate expanse of

Slow moving water
(did a trout start?)
and tumble on hands
and knees on the far

Bank to be greeted
by astonished rabbits,
like a parliament
of dwarfs, assembled

On their burrow-
eroded slope, endless
corridors down which
flashing scuts scatter.

2
Water ripple, grass growth,
smell of sorrel, watercress,
a bat flitting, hazel
and sally whispering.

A patient audience
for my hero feats,
testing the edge
for a sound take-off.

Secret training rites
to satisfy no command,
but the self-ordained
urge to perfection.

Evening after evening
practising, always
moving the marker
further down the river,

To find a wider
more impossible spot,
the ultimate leap
beyond Lynchs' meadow

(Rock girdled,
a deep, dark, circling
turnhole that could
swirl over my head).

A task to which I
slowly nerve myself
circling always nearer,
until late one night

Closing my eyes,
I take off, to find
myself on the far
ledge, scrabbling.

3
Secret wellsprings
of strength, forgotten
disciplines of night,
those long, lovely

Leaps in the dark
returning now to steady
my mind, nourish
my courage as

No longer young
I take your hand
to face a different
more frightening task,

Defying conventions
for love's sake,
leaving behind ground
tested and safe

Using a lesson learnt
long ago in Lynchs' meadow,
circling the task,
to vault the flow;

Taking off again
into the uncertain dark,
hoping to land safely
on a far, warm bank.

Harvest

That first wild summer
we watched each other,
my graying hair and
wary eyes slowly drawn
to be warmed by your
flaring hair, abundant body.

No ice princess, you call
me down from my high tower –
on our first night together
I awoke, to watch over
your rich shape, a shower
of gold in the moonlight.

And an old fable stirred:
a stag rising from a wet brake,
– Danae deluged by Zeus?
Rather, youth's promise fulfilled,
homely as a harvest field
from my Tyrone childhood

Where I hoist warm sheaves
to tent them into golden stooks,
each detail, as I wade
through the moonlit stubble,
crayon bright, as in
a child's colouring-book.

Above

Love transfixes me
with an accusing eye

– I have been angry
with you, all day,

ever since, clumsy,
suspicious, heavy-

footed, you recalled
the terms of our bargain

neither to put a halter
on either, bridle or bit.

But no sooner, my dear,
were you free of my arms,

dismounted, like any mortal,
from pommel and saddle,

than you renege, insist
on speaking anxiously

of houses, properties,
mortgages, marriages,

all that grid of society
we had glimpsed so gloriously

from above, but which again
seems to you necessary

as we float down to it.

Discords

1

There is a white light in the room.
It is anger. He is angry, or
She is angry, or both are angry.
To them it is absolute, total,
It is everything; but to the visitor,
The onlooker, the outsider,
It is the usual, the absurd;
For if they did not love each other
Why should they heed a single word?

2

Another sad goodbye at the airport;
Neither has much to say, *en garde*,
Lest a chance word turn barbed.
You bring me, collect me, each journey
Not winged as love, but heavy as duty;
Lohengrin's swan dipping to Charon's ferry.

3

A last embrace at the door,
Your lovely face made ugly
By a sudden flush of tears
Which tell me more than any phrase,
Tell me what I most need to hear,
Wash away and cleanse my fears:
You have never ceased to love me.

The Well-Beloved

To wake up and discover –
a *splairge* of chill water –
that she was but a forthright woman
on whom we had bestowed
(because of the crook of an elbow,
the swing of a breast or hip,
a glance, half-understood)
divinity or angelhood?

Raised by the fury of our need,
supplicating, lusting, grovelling
before the tall tree of Artemis,
the transfiguring bow of Diana,
the rooting vulva of Circe, or
the slim shape of a nymph,
luring, dancing, beckoning:
all her wild disguises!

And now she does not shine,
or ride, like the full moon,
gleam or glisten like cascades
of uncatchable, blinding water;
disturb, like the owl's cry,
predatory, hovering: marshlight,
moonstone, or devil's daughter,
but conducts herself like any

Ordinary citizen, orderly or slattern,
giving us a piece of her mind,
pacifying or scolding children,
or, more determinedly, driving
or riding to her office, after
depositing the children in a *crèche*,
while she fulfills herself,
competing with the best.

Of course, she is probably saying
the same thing of us, as Oisín,
our tall hero from Fairyland,
descends or falls from the saddle
to dwindle into an irritable husband,
worn down by the quotidian,
unwilling to transform the night
with love's necessary shafts of light.

Except that when the old desires stir
– fish under weed-tangled waters –
will she remember that we once were
the strange ones who understood
the powers that coursed so furiously
through her witch blood, prepared
to stand, bareheaded, open handed,
to recognise, worship and obey:

To defy custom, redeem the ordinary,
with trembling heart and obeisant knee
to kneel, prostrate ourselves again,
if necessary, before the lady?

She Cries

She puts her face against the wall
and cries, crying for herself,
crying for our children, crying
for all of us
                in this strange age
of shrinking space, with the needle
of Concorde saluting Mount Gabriel
with its supersonic boom, soaring
from London or Paris to Washington,
a slender, metallic, flying swan

and all the other paraphernalia, hidden
missiles hoarded in silos, bloated
astronauts striding the dusty moon,
and far beyond, our lonely message,
that long probe towards Venus

but most of all for her husband
she cries, against the wall,
the poet at his wooden desk,
that toad with a jewel in his head,
no longer privileged, but still
trying to crash, without faltering,
the sound barrier, the dying word.

Sibylle's Morning

1
She wakes in a hand-painted cot,
chats and chortles to herself,
a healthy small being, a happy elf,
sister to the early train whistle,
the bubbling dawn chorus along
the wisteria of Grattan Hill.

No complaints as yet, enjoying
through curtains the warm sunlight,
until she manages to upend herself.
Then the whine starts. Is it anger
or lust for the bottle?

Lift her up, warm and close
or held at arm's length –
that smell, like a sheep pen,
a country hedge steaming after rain.

As the bottle warms, the decibels increase,
the scaldie's mouth gapes open;
head numb, coated tongue,
cortex ends squealing, no
thirsty drunk at a bar,
nursing a hangover, manages such concentration.

Daughter, dig in, with fists like ferns
unfurling, to basic happiness!
Little one, you are now
nothing but the long music of the gut,
a tug of life, with halts
for breathing, stomach swelling.

2

On your throne afterwards
bang your heels, examine your new
and truly wonderful hands,
try out, warm up, your
little runs of satisfaction.

Day by day, they also grow,
sound experiments in the laboratory
of the self, animal happiness,
the tonal colour of rage, cartoon
attempts to communicate, eyes beaming,
burbles rising. Best of all when

like any bird or beast waking,
you wail to yourself, with whoops,
finger stuffed gurgles, and my reward
for the morning, your speciality,
(after the peristaltic hiccup)
when you smile and squeal with
sudden, sharp whistles –
O my human kettle!

Difference

I want, says Sibylle,
my small daughter,
at the big table.

You don't want,
says her lovely mother,
you would like

*and, besides, there
is another small
word, missing.*

Please, would like,
tries the rascal again,
playing it backwards

the silence between
depending on the ruddy
glow of the peach,

the size of the plum
small eyes measuring
the pleasures of opposition

against the necessity
to give in. *Would like,
please*, again.

Tea Ceremony

She brings us to her secret place, behind the apple tree, on the last terrace of our garden. Ordering her little friends bossily, she leads them first up the ladder; we follow behind, bashful giants. She has set up a table, a few boards balanced on stones, where a half-broken doll sits facing a bruised teddy. One by one, large and small, we are assigned our places: 'now *you* sit there' and '*you* sit here'.

Then a fresh batch of orders arrives. 'Since I'm the Mummy I pour out the tea.' A child's hand reaches out, plucks and distributes china cups so delicate that they are invisible. Then it grasps a teapot handle out of space and leans across to each of us in turn, before settling back that solid object made of air down in front of her. 'And here are the sandwiches and biscuits.' Each of us receives a dusty twig or leaf. 'Now you all eat up and if any of you complain I'll tell Daddy on you.' She gives Teddy an affectionate poke which sends him sprawling to the ground. 'And sit up straight: no slouching when we have visitors.'

Solemnly, we lift the cups to our lips, toasting each other silently. Through the branches of the apple tree we can see the city, a pall of smoke over the docks, the opaque matte surface of the River Lee. Beyond those small hills is the airport and as we drink invisibility a plane climbs, a sliver of silver in the sunlight. Filtered through the apple blossom its sound is as distant and friendly as the hum of a honey-seeking bee.

A Small Death

My daughter, Una, wanders
off to play in the forest,
unafraid, her new rag doll
clutched under one arm:
a small fairy queen, trail-
ed by her elderly knight.

At the centre, I find her
beneath black hemlock, red cedar,
halted on a carpet, a compost
of fallen leaves, rusty haws
and snowberries, knobbly chestnuts:
decay's autumnal weft.

She has found a dead bird
which she holds up in her
other hand; eyes, bright beads,
but the long beak spiky, cold,
twig legs crisped inwards.
Why not fly? she demands

And as I kneel to explain
(taking the retted corpse away)
dead, she repeats, puzzled.
So we bury the scant body
under a mound of damp leaves,
a gnome's pyre, a short barrow:

Her first funeral ceremony.
Home now, I nudge gently,
past the slapping branches,
the shallow Pacific rain pools
she loves ploutering through
in her diminutive wellingtons.

Beyond the tall woods, lights
of Victoria are flickering on:
yellow flares of sodium
under dark coastal clouds
crossing Vancouver Island;
dream cattle swaying home.

Phillipe

Deaf and dumb since his hapless birth,
Inside the echo chamber of his skull
He hears the grimace of grinding teeth;
His form of broken, internal speech.
And always he lifts white, sightless eyes
Towards all pulsing sources of light, skies
That warm his insistent, upraised face,
Airs that play around his naked body,
Waters that pour, caress, and bless until
He breaks, like a bird, into grateful cries.
Handsome as some damaged Gothic angel,
Fate has yet left him one startling skill,
A lithe torso he arches with fakir's grace
– Which may not spare his early disappearance.

Nest

When all the birds
    in the nest are there,
is that the start
    of a new despair?

The Broken Doll

O little broken doll, dropped in the well,
thrown aside by a child, scampering downhill
to hide under the skirts of his mother!
In twilight's quiet he took sudden fright
as toadstool caps snatched at his tongue,
foxgloves crooked their fingers at him
and from the oak, he heard the owl's low call.
His little heart almost stopped when a weasel
went by, with a fat young rabbit in its jaws,
loose guts spilling over the grass while
a bat wing flicked across the evening sky.

He rushed away so noisily and ever since
you are a lasting witness to the fairy arrow
that stabbed his ear; stuck in the mud
your plastic eyes squinny open from morning
to night: you see the vixen and her brood
stealing up to lap the ferny swamphole
near their den, the badger loping to wash
his paws, snuff water with his snout. On
Pattern days people parade seven clockwise
rounds; at every turn, throwing in a stone.

Those small stones rain down on you.
The nuts from the hazel tree that grows
to the right of the well also drop down:
you will grow wiser than any blessed trout
in this ooze! The redbreasted robin
of the Sullivans will come to transform
the surface to honey with her quick tail,

churn the depths to blood, but you don't move.
Bemired, your neck strangled with lobelias,
I see your pallor staring starkly back at me
from every swimming hole, from every pool, Ophelia.

after the Irish of Nuala Ní Dhomhnaill

Migrant Poet

I was in Dalcais from Mayday,
Until every bush shed its wisp of down,
Now I head north to stay from Samhain
Until the cuckoo calls from the royal *dun*.

Listen, the brent goose wings across the sea,
Salmon sleep in the clear, cold stream.
Every bird seeks its winter quarters.
I'll not stir, till summer comes again.

after the Early Irish

Scotia

i. m. Hugh MacDiarmid

We have come so far north,
farther than we have ever been
to where gales strip everything
and the names ring guttural
syllables of old Norse:
Thurso, Scrabster, Laxdale,
names clang like a battle-axe.

Then further west. There beauty
softens, a darkening estuary,
Farr or Borgie or Skerray where
waist-high in shallow waters
silent shadows cast at night
to lassoo the lazily feeding trout
to gleam upon our hotel plate.

Still farther, mountains gather,
blue peak lifting beyond blue peak,
Ben Loyal and then Ben Hope,
noble, distant as the Twelve Bens
or Brandon; single tracks on
endless moors, or threading along
the flanks of melancholy lochs.

Loch Loyal and Loch Naver,
where Alpine flowers blossom,
the wilderness's blessing;
as MacDiarmid will proudly remark
in our last, rambling conversation,
'strange, lovely things grow up there,
ecologically, *vairy* inter-resting.'

By such roads, only sheep prosper,
bending to crop the long acre, or
whiten the heather, like bog cotton.
The name of this county, Sutherland,
synonym for burnings, clearances
the black aura of Castle Dunrobbin,
stone cottages broken, like Auburn.

Along the new motorway, trucks
and trailers strain, an invasion
grinding from England, the Grampians
pushed aside, in search of wealth;
the North Sea's blackening pulse,
the rigs towed from Moray Firth
to prop a fading British strength.

Beyond Tongue, still rises Ben Hope
and that star of mountains, Suilven,
that beckons to an intent fisherman,
MacCaig, with whom I share a patronym.
His unswerving eye and stylish line
pierce through flesh to dying bone.
May Scotland always have such fishermen

Nourishing a lonely dream of how
this desolate country might have been!
The rightful arrogance of MacDiarmid's
calling together of Clann Albann,
or the surging lamentations of MacLean,
the sound of his echoing Gaelic
a fierce pibroch crying on the wind.

A Ballad for Berryman

John, a letter or a song
to celebrate our heady hours together;
memories to warm this filthy Irish weather,
of that long dreepy Dublin winter
we both had to suffer.

Hot toddies in Beggar's Bush
while you decanted another rush
or run of your fermenting *Dream Songs*.
I was still young, aghast at genius,
concerned about your happiness,

Finding a place, pals for the evening,
a practical hero-worshipper, only half understanding
your long turmoil or *hegira*
from our first meeting in Iowa
to Jack Ryan's barn-like bar.

Soon after, you came through Paris,
blundered your way up the Rue Daguerre.
To Esteban, working under his cameo of Baudelaire,
you slowly pronounced, in stentorian French:
'ou est le poète Irlandais?'

And Claude soft-footed across the way:
*'il y a un Moïse Americain
qui te demande.'* Behold, behind him
then your great beard appeared; Henry,
grinning from ear to ear.

Peninsula

Places where few come
mother earth sprouts
her natural defences;
jagged yellow gorse,
poison ivy and oak,
tugging, tangled briars.

Beneath harsh brambles
a hoard of blackberries,
swarthy gouts of juice.
Under crimson skirts
of fuchsia, bees hover
to cling for nectar.

Creaking crabs' claws
defend warm coves;
translucent parachutes
of stinging jellyfish
(flaccid heart valves,
pulsing, expanding).

Bladders of seawrack
lift to disclose a
skyblue bed of mussels:
spiky urchins crouch
in yellow rockpools.
Pursed oysters drowse.

To drift, lazily,
scarcely disturbing
the tidal rhythms,
kin to the waterstrider,
keeping company with
a shoal of fish.

Feathery pines, below
long folded mountains;
the light always shifting.
On a seaweeded rock
a solemnity of gulls,
chattering, staring.

An act of attention
as when swaying home
from the spring well
with a brimming bucket;
its trembling meniscus,
water's hymen.

To stand stockstill
until a butterfly
alights on your arm,
steadying small sails;
scarlet spots upon
an ochre ground.

Dame Nature's self-
delighting richness;
in a clump of iris
a grasshopper shrills.
In the midge thick twilight
a sea trout flails, while

Abruptly in the bay
a school of dolphin
rehearse their turns,
thrashing the water
with their flat tails,
exultant watermills!

The Black Lake

Across the black lake
Two figures row their boat
With slow, leaning strokes.
The grind of their rowlocks
Is rhythmic as a heartbeat.

Seven stooks stand
In a moonwashed field –
Seven pillars of gold –
While beyond, two haystacks
Roped down to the earth.

Three lean cattle munch
The heavy aftergrass, or
Raise their heads towards
A stonewalled corner where
A couple lean from each other.

The moon climbs the hill.
The night brims with light,
A pantry, silent with milk.
The rowers reach the cottage,
The couple do not speak.

Luggala

for Garech Browne

I

Again and again in dream, I return to that shore. There is a wind rising, a gull is trying to skim over the pines, and the waves whisper and strike along the bright sickle of the little strand. Shoving through reeds and rushes, leaping over a bogbrown stream, I approach the temple by the water's edge, death's shrine, cornerstone of your sadness. I stand inside, by one of the pillars of the mausoleum, and watch the water in the stone basin. As the wind ruffles cease, a calm surface appears, like a mirror or crystal. And into it your face rises, sad beyond speech, sad with an acceptance of blind, implacable process. For by this gray temple are three tombs, a baby brother, a half-sister and a grown brother, killed at twenty-one. Their monuments of Wicklow granite are as natural here as the scattered rocks, but there is no promise of resurrection, only the ultimate silence of the place, the shale littered face of the scree, the dark, dark waters of the glacial lake.

II

The road leading from the white wedding cake of the hunting lodge is lined with late blooming daffodils. As you leave, it fades back into its mountain setting, a folly nestling under boulder-strewn granite cliffs, with a stream rushing down by its side. Under the trunk of each tree, flowers shelter, and there is a path leading down to the lake. You push open a wooden gate and a herd of deer starts away, ears pricked, eyes alert, nimble-legged. Then they halt at a distance, tensely shy, but curious. The path twists and turns, following bends of the bogbrown stream. In the wooden hollow of the boathouse you pull and tug ropes until the boat descends with a splash into dark, lapping waters. Oar blades rise and fall and soon you are at the heart of the lake with the hills forming a circle, you the centre.

III

But you are not alone: a noise disturbs you, rhythmic as the beat of oars. A mother swan is teaching her young to fly: round and round in that protecting silence they turn, necks timidly outstretched, wings slowly beating. Now and again one falls, breaking its reflection in the lake, then struggling upwards to join its fellows. And then you realise there is another, still greater presence. Motionless and gray, the huge cliff hangs upsidedown in the mirror of the lake; water, mountain and forest held in lasting embrace.

Mount Eagle

1
The eagle looked at this changing world;
sighed and disappeared into the mountain.

Before he left he had a last reconnoitre:
the multi-coloured boats in the harbour

nodded their masts and a sandy white
crescent of strand smiled back at him.

How he liked the slight, drunk lurch
of the fishing fleet, the tide hoist-

ing them a little, at their ropes' end.
Beyond, wrack, and the jutting rocks

emerging, slowly, monsters stained
and slimed with strands of seaweed.

Ashore, beached boats and lobster-
pots, settled as hens in the sand.

2
Content was life in its easiest form;
another was the sudden growling storm

which the brooding eagle preferred,
bending his huge wings into the winds'

wild buffeting, or thrusting down along
the wide sky, at an angle, slideways

to survey the boats, scurrying homewards,
tacking against the now contrary winds,

all of whom he knew by their names.
To be angry in the morning, calmed

by midday, but brooding again in
the evening was all in a day's quirk

with lengthy intervals for silence,
gliding along, like a blessing, while

the fleet toiled on earnestly beneath
him, bulging with a fine day's catch.

3
But now he had to enter the mountain.
Why? Because a cliff had asked him?

The whole world was changing, with one
language dying; and another encroaching,

bright with buckets, cries of children.
There seemed to be no end to them,

and the region needed a guardian –
so the mountain had told him. And

a different destiny lay before him:
to be the spirit of that mountain.

Everyone would stand in awe of him.
When he was wrapped in the mist's caul

they would withdraw because of him,
peer from behind blind or curtain.

When he lifted his wide forehead
bold with light, in the morning,

they would all laugh and smile with him.
It was a greater task than an eagle's

aloofness, but sometimes, under his oilskin
of coiled mist, he sighs for lost freedom.

Knockmany

You do not forget
and I always come back.
Stepping from the car
outside Clogher, I saw
a brilliant rainbow
lifting its prismatic arch
across Knockmany Hill
as in a healing dream
in savage Chicago. It
shone both a secret
and a sacrament, a promise
and its fulfillment.
I still live by it.

The Hill of Silence

I
From the platform
of large raised stones

lines appear to lead us
along the hillside

bog tufts softening
beneath each step

bracken and briar
restraining our march

clawing us back, slowing
us to perception's pace.

II
A small animal halts,
starts, leaps away

and a lark begins
its dizzy, singing climb

towards the upper skies
and now another stone appears

ancient, looming, mossed
long ago placed,

lifted to be a signpost
along the old path.

III
Let us climb further.
As one thought leads
to another, so one lich-

ened snout of stone
still leads one on,
beckons to a final one.

IV
Under its raised slab
thin trickles of water

gather to a shallow pool
in which the head stone

mirrors, and rears
to regard its shadow self,

and a diligent spider weaves
a trembling, silver web

a skein of terrible delicacy
swaying to the wind's touch

a fragile, silken scarf
a veined translucent leaf.

V
This is the slope of loneliness.
This is the hill of silence.
This is the winds' fortress.
Our world's polestar.
A stony patience.

VI

We have reached a shelf
that surveys the valley

on these plains below
a battle flowed and ebbed

and the gored, spent warrior
was ferried up here

where water and herbs
might staunch his wounds.

VII

Let us also lay ourselves
down in this silence

let us also be healed
wounds closed, senses cleansed

as over our bowed heads
the mad larks multiply

needles stabbing the sky
in an ecstasy of stitching fury

against the blue void
while from clump and tuft

cranny and cleft, soft footed
curious, the animals gather around.

Survivor

Under his high cliff, Fintan waited.
He watched as the floods rose, rose,
Never fell. He heard the women wail,
Wail, and accept. He felt the change
Through his nostrils, flattening to gills,
His arms thinning to fins, his torso
Tightening into a single thrash:
The undulating flail of a great fish.

Nothing human would last. For centuries
He slept at the bottom of the world,
Currents stroking his sleek, strong back.
Slowly, the old bare earth reappeared,
Barren, but with a rainbow brightened.
Life might begin again. He lunges upwards.